Praise
I Believe, and J

"Ms. Glyckherr is a true and very talented poet. Her words come directly from the heart. She writes about what she knows and writes with a true and humble passion. The mark of a great poet. I love her work!"

Jay Snider
Oklahoma Poet Laureate 2023-2024
Academy of Western Artists Poetry Recording of the Year 2006
Academy of Western Artists Poet of the Year 2008

****

"P.S. Glyckherr puts her heart and soul on the page for readers who have the good fortune to discover her well-crafted and well-lived poetry. Emily Elizabeth Dickinson, her mentor, would be pleased to see how she inspired this author's poetry. We embark with Glyckherr on a journey across pain and pleasure, love and loss and ever back to family and faith. From "Rusted Clean" through "After the Rain" and beyond—not just words, but images, feelings and sensations speak of a well-earned Sage Stage. Having poems preserved inside the cover of a beautiful book shows us a wise woman who has truly claimed an Epic Encore. You will treasure your copy of *I Believe & Jesus Knows!*"

Beth Harkins
Storyteller, author of *The Possibility of Everywhere: Casablanca to Oklahoma City, Katmandu to Timbuktu*
Facilitator of "Passport to Your Epic Encore: for Sage Stage Women Ready to Live Vitally, Connect Deeply and Share Boldly in This, Their One Precious Life." http://www.bethharkins.com

© 2024 P.S. Glyckherr

Published by Atmosphere Press

Cover design by Felipe Betim

No part of this book may be reproduced without permission from the author except in brief quotations and in reviews.

Atmospherepress.com

For my daughters and their children

Contents

I Believe 1

Outside the Lines 2

My Coloring Book 3

Orientation to Life 4

Once I Was a Runner! 5

Seasons 6

The Photograph 7

Sweet Music 8

Emily Elizabeth Dickinson 9

Rusted Clean 10

Extraordinary 11

If I Were a Clown 12

After the Rain 13

Grandmother's Day 14

Port of Call 15

Proof of Love 16

Remembering 17

Emily's Vineyard 18

Megan's Voice 19

Ribbons, Pearls, Cars, and Dolls 20

Thanksgiving! 21

Oh, Christmas Tree 22

Butterfly in White 23

Butterfly Song 24

Evergreen 25

Piece of Your Heart 26

Friendship	27
Location Theory	28
Prospect Theory	29
Heart of a Yellow Rose	30
About Mary – The Chosen	31
Holy Differences	32
Real Love	33
Fruits of the Spirit	34
Gift from God	35
Perfection	36
Thoughts of Eternity	37
Sensibility	38
Snowflake at Sea	39
The Sailor	40
Parts of Hallelujah	41
It Was Sunday	42
Goodbyes	43
Life After Jackson	44
A Useful Shower	45
Comfort Prayer	46
Still	47
Unfinished Blessings	48
My Will	49
Passenger and Pilot	50
Angel	51
Jesus Knows	52

I Believe

I believe in the Baby Jesus –
God's Cherished and Only Son,
Who grew up to face the Cross –
to suffer and die for Everyone!
He endured our sins and sorrows
beneath a crown of thorns.
Then He rose again,
so we could be reborn!
I believe in a Resurrected Savior –
with Whom I'll live one day!
Though it's hard to conceive
He'd want someone like me ...
He does! And I Believe!

Outside the Lines

I first colored "outside the lines"
before the age of three.
Daddy disappeared. Momma broke down.
There was no phone, no food, no LOVE to be found.
I sat there and cried the biggest tears,
soaking my picture – turning black lines to blue.
Three kids were alone. That was all I knew.
There was nowhere for little ones to go alone.
There was nowhere for us to hide.
There was no way to color inside the lines
or toss all my tears aside.
But then came a loud knock at the door!
Could it be a friend?
Our grandparents – our "godsend" –
packed us up and took us home with them!
Though Momma would never again be fine,
I did learn to color "inside those lines."
But I will forever remember the fear I felt
before real LOVE arrived – just in time!

My Coloring Book

On the blank page of my life
I brushed a stage
slanted upward toward the sky!
Painted it red ... not blue,
blushed in Apple-blossom hue –
I don't know why ... I have NO clue!
But from under those shadings of
ruby and ruddy smudge
rose fruits worth consuming
with only God to judge.

Orientation to Life

Mastering "life" requires constant learning –
every day for as long as we live!
Without it, we will not know success or
our capability to win.
We must give ourselves permission to fail.
Set tired boats afloat to sail –
even when the water's rough.
In maneuvering life's toughest turns,
our faith can be enough.
We must wrap ourselves in God's Armor
with no chance of giving up … or in.
So, when we find ourselves falling,
He can lift us up again!

Once I Was a Runner!

Once upon a time in the 20th Century ...
I was a Runner!
I ran the fifty-yard dash faster than most of my friends!
I broad jumped, popped the tether ball ...
hooped those baskets and was the
best can-kicker of all.
I jogged well into my forties –
even after breaking a leg!
But more than anything else, I just loved to RUN!
I simply LOVED to RACE!!
But today I don't run anymore ... or race.
Instead, I take small, decisive steps ...
and not at all with grace.
Sometimes I even stumble and fall –
then pretend I'm totally fine
with this new stance in life,
but the truth of it is ...
I miss the wind blowing through my hair ... and
the rush of my heart at the finish line!
Yes, I was once a Runner!
I ached to RACE!
Once upon a time.

Seasons

Leaves are falling –
yellow, orange, and brown.
All green will soon be gone ...
moving on to Winter's window.
Frozen tears tumbling down
make me love the Springtime –
minus the storms.
Awaiting Summer gardens now,
warm with sun-filled food and flowers.
Counting down the hours 'til
Autumn leaves fall once more.

The Photograph

You feel a little lonely, don't you, Dad?
Smokin' those same old scenes
of "all those things" you COULD have had.
Three times you strolled down the aisle –
pretending each time you might begin to care ...
while thinkin' out loud,
"If only I could have stayed there a while –
If only I could have BEEN THERE."
Four children – ALIVE!
And each one survived you,
despite your rejection of perfect news.
But good news was just a game back then
with rules too much for you.
I don't hate you, Dad ... I never did.
The truth is: I just don't know you!
And if I had, would I have even CALLED you Dad?
And would I have ever KNOWN the truth?
Many times, I held this ONE tiny photo
tightly inside my hands ...
while pretending not to see all the others
shredded alongside my mother's empty bed.
It was hard to ignore her mournful pain and
my innocent fear of her dying
while you were dismembered again and again!
Some select and silent scars still simmer now alone ...
after a lifetime allotted to heal,
and still ...
those old wounds wander out
in search of that LOVE I have tried to find
in that ONE ragged photo left behind.
Far, far beyond the VOID I will forever feel ...
This is ALL I have
to prove YOU WERE REAL.

Sweet Music

Like a sunflower, strong in the desert heat, or
a wildflower rising from a coup of weeds …
like a crystal-blue waterfall pouring fresh and clear
or a "white-tailed kite" rocking his sphere,
I have grown up with you. I rise with you!
My heart is wide-open to my confidant and friend.
You have inspired me, strengthened me, and
repeatedly refreshed my soul.
Thank you, Sweet Music!
Please never let me go.

Emily Elizabeth Dickinson

I wanted to write like Emily –
in a unique, unconventional style.
Though no one can write
like Emily wrote –
my effort still makes me smile.
I named my first-born Emily.
Then Elizabeth came along.
And in every moment spent with them,
my heart's been filled with song!
Though I will never be the Poet
Ms. Dickinson is known to be,
I will always treasure her secrets
sown deep inside of me.

Rusted Clean

"Good" can be hidden in angry hearts,
longing for peace –
to make a fresh start.
Fashioned from sorrow on tender ground,
I stood there alone ...
No pity, no sound.
For I had already tasted every sad phrase and
greeted the ending of those rusted days.
I crushed all the hate left in my way –
clearing a path for PEACE to stay.
And, finally, I was clean!

Extraordinary

Free me from mere convention!
Do not restrain me, please!
For all that I am is not realized
resting safely on my knees.
Let me DANCE through every rainbow!
Let me FLY beyond darkness ...
and leap fearful seas!
Smell each petal of every flower,
count each color in the butterfly's wing.
I long for fertile discovery –
to delight in ALL LIVING THINGS.
To welcome God's arrival
when we will ALL stand and sing!
Free me from simple standards.
Save me from strict routines.
Grant me ALL THINGS INCREDIBLE!
LIFE is no ORDINARY thing!

If I Were a Clown

If I were a clown in this big old town,
I could be anything I choose.
In costume and makeup –
my disguise could surprise, and
I might make the local news.
A woman or man, a tiger or lamb,
timid or bold, youthful ... or old,
and without even saying two words –
with just one gesture from my lips,
my jokes could still be heard.
Whether chubby or skinny, frowning or grinning,
I could always be winning my race.
And no matter how stunning or surprising I am,
a child could color my face.

After the Rain

Smell the air after the rain.
Breathe in that scent ...
spend just a moment –
a moment well-spent.
Take it all in.
Flowers wait.
No, not ready for my hair to turn gray ...
then white –
unprepared for changes in my life.
But at least I've learned
how to enjoy the flowers
after the rain.

Grandmother's Day

You gave up your heart long ago –
loved a child you didn't know.
My protector, my teacher,
my biggest fan ...
you helped me become
all that I am.
Your love has been endless,
so selfless and kind, and
I thank my God that
HE made YOU ... MINE.
Only He could create,
without further thought,
someone who'd love me
for all that I'm not!

Port of Call
(for Gary Bob)

You will always be my "Port of Call" –
that place I stop to unload despair –
release all cares and leave them there.
You repair my mind! You mend my soul!
I leave fear behind
because I know –
I am yours and you are mine.
Over mountains of waves, I will happily climb
in gratitude for this chosen time, and
I'll honor each moment you give for free.
Because of you, I can be me.

Proof of Love
(for Em)

I stopped caffeine – just for you!
Ate healthy food in place of scraps I'd choose.
Consumed so much water – though I hated the taste!
Took naps and tried to watch my waist.
Prepared for lengthy labor and pain.
Drove miles through traffic and pounding rain
so that you'd arrive here safe and sound, and
I thought ... a deeper love could never be found!
But on YOUR day, my life profoundly changed ...
when I discovered a new kind of LOVE –
and I would never be the same!
I listened for your every movement
and your every tiny cry.
And as I sang to you every word of every lullaby,
I discovered that "Mother's Miracle" –
the one meant just for me ...
an innocent, promising kind of LOVE
from a child that I could see –
like a delicate sculpture uniquely styled
in a garden of flowers growing wild!

Remembering
(for Meg Elizabeth)

I'll always remember that first time we met –
so tiny, so fragile ... it was frightening!
And yet, the first time we danced –
You were just three.
The music was soft, and I was down on my knees.
When you first tied your shoes, you shouted ... then cried.
Some things were hard, but you always tried.
I'll forever remember the first time you sang ... and
how you LAUGHED OUT LOUD
at most any old thing.
When we danced at your wedding and
gave you away ...
you were the LOVELIEST vision
on your HAPPIEST day!
You've been a true JOY to me
all through your years –
through countless "Firsts" and
through each of my fears.
I can clearly recall that first time we met –
and though you've turned FORTY,
I still can't forget.

Emily's Vineyard

She must paint both day and night,
yes, every night and every day –
while she sleeps and when she prays.
For a Vineyard grows inside her heart
from tiny seeds creating art.
Like grapes growing wild to make fine wine,
she brushes insistently across the pine
onto canvas lips that drink it all down
fueling the feast soon to be found ...
a flourishing soul on her battleground.

Megan's Voice

Her cry is reserved for only a few –
to those with a friendship point of view.
And when she sings, the sun shines so high ...
above all the clouds floating by.
But when she laughs, she "cackles"!
Everyone hears her JOY!
It's the sound of satisfaction
No one can destroy!

Ribbons, Pearls, Cars, and Dolls

Better ...
than the memory of a young girl
wearing a crown of brightly colored ribbons
flowing down her hair, and
a boy in a pearly-white vest
driving his mother's Catalina best
to the prom,
BEAUTIFUL THINGS ...
keep happening to ME!
I was told the news –
THRILLING to believe!
Then, a GRANDCHILD was born,
and I began to imagine
those brightly colored ribbons and
pearls leaping from the sea!
I became a "GRANDMOTHER" –
not just once or twice,
but again, and again –
and many MORE times again!
These "BIG DOLLS" arrived
in their very own time –
reawakening thrills in me!
But, instead of speeding on past them,
now I intentionally STOP ...
to listen for those exquisite words
they just might say!
They fill my mind with such attitude!
I'm astonished by my gratitude
whenever they come to PLAY.
And as I take the time to ponder
all the miracles of LOVE
life has offered me for free –
These are the "GRANDEST" of surprises
God has granted me.

Thanksgiving!

Almighty
God
Omnipotent
Supremely
Outstanding
Stunningly
Magnificent
Wonderful
Around ALL
Is Good
...Thanksgiving!
Good is
ALL around
Wonderful
Magnificent
Stunningly
Outstanding
Supremely
Omnipotent
God
Almighty

Oh, Christmas Tree

God created this lovely tree –
every Holly Berry Leaf waiting just for me.
And as I decorate, I celebrate
the many blessings handed down
in colors of His Rainbows
now twinkling all around.
Other bright and shining trimmings –
in Christmas red and gold
properly grace a Nativity scene
where His humble story's told.
And as I climb the ladder now
to place a Star atop my tree,
I thank God for HIS ONLY SON –
born to rescue me.

Butterfly in White

Silent and graceful –
like the dancing heart of an Angel
delivering peace from a departed soul,
our JOY begins
when we accept our freedom
to cherish ALL WONDERS –
both large and small –
for when we are COMPLETE,
We will have known them all!

Butterfly Song

Life is full of bickering and blame –
a sometimes-senseless game of surviving
that constant censure,
spoiling all life's adventures and
turning sweet days into shame.
Why not just be kind?
Climb a little higher
than we did the day before?
Kick out all the fires and
blow them out the door!
We've all heard those songs
about pain and dying.
Why not remember the Butterflies FLYING ...
and landing safely on our privileged windowsills?
For until we clearly see
what the gift of LIFE really means,
we won't ENJOY the Butterflies!

Evergreen

GRACE –
has wide-open arms!
Sacred skies have shown me this.
There is no higher place,
so how can I resist
HIS PERFECTION –
wrapped in yellow sunsets
resting on holy streets of gold?
Told all my life about
the EVERGREEN –
constant, never changing.
And as I look –
EVERYWHERE...
I can see
GOD
is
ALIVE,
and He shelters my soul!

Piece of Your Heart

I still remember that first smile you gave
and your distinctively quiet laughter ...
after eating something HOT!
It was NOT just the sound of your voice –
but your purest tenor that made my choice
not to be alone.
Guarded, you opened yourself to me, and
I saw a rarely seen work of art.
Then much, much more than I deserved,
you served me a piece of your heart!

Friendship

It seems I've known you all my life –
my most devoted friend.
You're like the sister I never knew –
like a kinship without end!
Because God saw potential
in the hearts of you and me,
He brought us both together and
caused us both to see ...
we can open our hearts to be inspired,
to speak our minds
in the most incredible ways, and
still embrace our friendship
on our most distressing days.
I think I'll forever be drawn to you –
the truest friend I've come to know, and
I am honored by your love ...
a marvel, a wonder –
a miracle all our own.

Location Theory

The where and the why things happen
are often intriguing to me.
If we unwind the string, peel away
all layers of mystery in unexpected things,
we'll discover that ONE line spoken,
or that ONE tired and broken wing.
I flew my kite on a sunny beach
while the mountains were calling for you.
Location Theory lingers
in most everything we do!

Prospect Theory

Prospect Theory assumes much about behavior games.
It's hard to explain, but no two people think the same.
"They say" we make choices based on gain – not loss,
but considering all personal risk –
differing from most of the rest,
well, predicting the costs for you or for me
is implausible at best.
Oh God, I do love Chocolate Cake –
a majorly predictable plus!
Though when it's planted on my thighs,
my costs are disgusting enough
that I might make a different choice …
one based on loss – not gain.
But Chocolate Cake without frosting?
It just wouldn't be the same!

Heart of a Yellow Rose

Dramatic Red or Passionate Pink?
Only good for some, I think.
But a Yellow Rose –
like the warmth of the Sun –
is meant to enlighten everyone!
If you greet a friend with a Yellow Rose,
don't be surprised if that friendship grows.
For there is power in the act of giving –
the way God's children should be living!
So, share some "Yellow" today with a friend.
Witness the spirit of JOY begin!

About Mary – The Chosen

The Mother of Jesus –
brave and kind.
"Beloved of God"
unafraid to find ...
beauty in her destiny.
No praise was sought.
No fame was bought ...
but with dreaded words spoken,
her heart fully broken –
she watched her son be crucified!
A Virgin – chosen by God Himself
to birth His Only Son.
And just one higher request
asked of anyone.

Holy Differences

We feel different from anyone else
because we are!
We don't fit in with everyone else
because we can't!
God made each of us
to stand out with conviction –
with purposeful, uniquely precious
differences ... that
only He could make possible.
Holy differences are sublime!
Each one of us is
"One-of-a-Kind"!

Real Love

The Bible says
"Love is patient, love is kind."
Guess that's why it's so hard to find.
"Love does not envy; love does not boast" –
taught to ALL Sinners, coast to coast!
"Love is not selfish, keeps no records of wrongs."
Guess that's why it takes so long
to hear our Maker's call –
to know the REAL meaning of LOVE at all.
"Love hopes, trusts, protects and preserves" –
A PERFECT Gift from the God we serve ...
and much, much more than we deserve.

Fruits of the Spirit

Fruits of the Spirit look much like JESUS –
healthy, clean, and new!
Planted for progress by God Himself –
something no one else can do.
As HE prepares HIS garden,
He weeds away all sin, and
clears a path to come ALIVE –
where peace and JOY move in!
The Store of the Lord –
is full of Gifts –
patience, kindness, and faith!
He tenderly offers us self-control …
served with His mercy and grace!

Gift from God

Truthfully ...
as I think a lot about
all the things I've got,
about all I've been taught ... and
treasuring MOST friendships I've sought,
still, I could call myself
"a little rotten to the core" –
though I know I'm better now
than I ever was before –
before I started thinking about
this BIG world I've long since known ... and
how exceedingly small I am, but
how very much I've grown!
I've discovered grateful thoughts are learned –
not earned, and
wisdom can't be bought –
it's discerned!
So, whenever I find light in the darkness,
harmony in the noise, or peace in the lion's den,
I STOP ... and SHOUT MY HEART OUT!
For I am so very, very GRATEFUL
for my WONDERFUL LIFE –
a GIFT from GOD, NO DOUBT!

Perfection

Perfection is NOT my intention.
No human is perfect nor ever could be.
What a waste to imply
I could FLY high above the clouds
on a stormy day.
But on my knees in contemplation –
with gratitude and admiration,
I find myself in that perfect place
to ease my weary mind –
on top of the HIGHEST MOUNTAIN
I never had to climb!

Thoughts of Eternity

How many years are left unborn?
My early years show up now and then
in random thoughts or in words I've said or heard,
and in all those places I've been.
When I hear simple music playing in the car,
I wonder just how long or far I must travel
to feel God's Endless LOVE!
As I reflect on all my days gone by –
celebrating God's promise
for my ETERNAL LIFE –
I can't help but ponder ...
phenomena I've not yet seen,
and ask the same question all over again:
How many years are still unborn
before HE shows me what HE means?

Sensibility

I've seen the SUN RISE ...
over snowy-white mountain tops.
I've heard the MUSIC of MOZART
playing from a stage.
I've smelled LILACS in BLOOM
on a crisp, spring morning and have
tasted Luxury CHOCOLATE –
laced generously with Sage.
I've sensed the INNOCENCE
in my Newborns' hands –
resting softly inside of mine.
And, if I could ask for ONE final blessing,
I would hope to feel LOVE again ...
one more time.

Snowflake at Sea

How many ships sail the sea each day –
seemingly sailing alone, and
single Snowflakes fall –
some large, some small,
uniquely on their own?
All souls find worth from a Savior
Who is always in command; and
though just one Snowflake at sea,
I am vital to my Captain's plan.
So, every day as WE sail away –
Joyful and unafraid,
I will praise His Holy Name –
for I am remarkably and wonderfully made.

The Sailor

We sail great ships –
boats with ruffled wings,
with singing bells
swinging over bopping buoys
and many more conspicuous things.
Yes, great, great ships –
crafted for much larger oceans,
unlike those inland waters that harbor
simple, scarce emotions.
We ebb and flow, reflect, grow and
burn what's left behind.
Then we take another look
to find that one significant sign –
Saying "Well done, Great Sailor.
Finally, you've arrived!"

Parts of Hallelujah

Which of my cries does God listen for?
Is it my perfect adoration call
from a poem or hymn of praise?
Is it my weeping doubt, my whimpering heart,
the voice of my struggles –
that broken Hallelujah part?
I believe He smiles ...
when He hears music coming from my voice –
in songs of gratitude and joy, but
what does He feel when I express my pain,
when I'm feeling all alone – like the devil's toy,
or when I've taken His name in vain?
When my thoughts wear me down and
I've looked all around for a change ... not to be found,
or when tragic events have taken their toll, or
when I've finally lost all control,
Who do I run to for solace, to renew my heart ... my soul?
I believe He is listening for my humble voice –
and whether I shout or whisper His name ...
I will always be HIS CHILD, and
that part will NEVER change!

It Was Sunday

It was Sunday when I got the call.
I was paralyzed with emotion.
I thought ... but I was just there ... and
we were just talking about ... and
we were listening to the Carolers
singing down the hall, and
she was making her plans ...
to go home and all.
That one person in all the world
I could count on was gone –
and not just to the grocery store, but
headed off to Heaven's shore!
When I first imagined her lying there
so stiff and cold ...
well, it stole my breath away!
But I knew she'd found her peace, and
I would see her again one day.
Knowing she'll be waiting for me
has helped me let her go.
It happened on a Sunday.
I wanted you to know.

Goodbyes

Life's a series of moments we use
to celebrate ...
with loved ones we choose.
Don't waste one gift!
NOT ONE can repeat!
Make every word count!
Make all hearts complete!
If this is the last time
you'll hold someone tight,
give them your best ...
and make love survive!

Life After Jackson

Afterwards,
I watched people moving
in slow motion past me ...
smiling, laughing
as though nothing had changed.
Life remains the same for them
while I fear I'll never smile again.
Hearing familiar music played?
Personally, I just must say
that its sweetness soured in my ears.
Do you think in a couple thousand years
I could listen once again ...
without so many tears?

A Useful Shower

A shower is useful in many ways.
It cleans away our physical grime and
calms our aches and pains.
It can wash away the tears we save
only for ourselves.
Sometimes it hurts way too much
to share them with anyone else.
When the water stops flowing and
all my thoughts are still,
I grab a fluffy towel and
create a forward will ...
to survive –
even though before my shower,
I barely felt alive.

Comfort Prayer

Watch over us, Lord, in times of loss.
You paid for our pain that day on the Cross.
Your gift of assurance – so selflessly made
allows us to live each day unafraid.
Comfort us, Lord, in times of distress.
You took ALL our worst and gave us your best.
Thank you, Lord, for taking our pain –
that day on the Cross, and again and again.
Be patient, Lord Jesus, with each of our cares.
We're becoming aware YOU are always there!

Still
(for Jackson Cash)

Still weaving those threads
of every word we've said
while memories of your smiles
are shared between my heart and lips ...
unequipped to comprehend
just how to mend or to
understand the purpose of
Seasons that appear –
rolling in and going out
the same time each year.
Yet I hope you know, my love,
I am here – thinking of you,
and missing you ...
still.

Unfinished Blessings

How many blessings go unfinished, I wonder?
Thundering disagreements –
the weight of words said in vain.
Pain destroys our senses.
Anger breaks our heart strings.
When we choose not to care
or not to share,
we leave broken blessings ...
Everywhere!
If a chance to bless another
remains unfinished,
God's love is postponed ...
His blessings unknown –
A cross we all must bear!

My Will

I never wanted to write my WILL.
To do so was to admit that one day
I will not write anything at all!
Quite appalling to think that
my thoughts wouldn't matter ...
and even sadder that no one
would be eating my burgers or fudge,
sipping my sodas, making me laugh –
while sharing our moments in photographs.
No one would think to invite me to lunch,
and much, much worse – that death of touch
and that rush of emotion when my children smiled.
I will miss those gifts my life here provides
while we're all together on earth – ALIVE!
And one day as they read my WILL,
I hope they realize I will love them "like this" ...
until there is no earth, no moon, no sky, and
no reason to write or say goodbye!

Passenger and Pilot

Life was aimlessly passing me by, and
I wondered why –
what is it God wants me to see?
And then I embraced His mountaintop
clearly in front of me!
Could I take the chance –
to follow my dreams without a single fear?
Then "The Pilot of My Future" said –
"Bring it home, child. Leave it here!"
So, I faced my new life with purpose
since I was no longer blind!
No more a casual Passenger here …
"The Pilot" had opened my eyes!
I recognized how Supreme
Eternal Life would be … and
why I should never compromise
God's perfect plan for me.
As Passengers, we depend on a Pilot
to guide us safely home.
This Pilot gave His life for me,
and I will kneel before His Throne!

Angel

I imagine the touch
of an Angel's hands, and
that eases my pain somehow.
I know I'm not the same.
I see the changes now.
I ache so much more ...
in places I never knew before!
I've become irrelevant to the future here –
like a short story someone might tell.
And though I may have more to give,
I have nothing left to sell.
It's no wonder why we welcome death –
refreshing, renewing – like a newborn's breath ...
where our chosen berth –
restored without command,
includes spotless, white linen ... and
pillows plumped up by an Angel's hands.

Jesus Knows

Jesus – the "Gentleman" –
though He shows us His LOVE
time and time again,
we still fail to fathom
our most FAITHFUL Friend!
True friends FORGIVE!
True friendship SURVIVES –
each mistake we make
each day of our lives.
With HIS LOVE Everlasting,
we have much time to grow, and
I am truly thankful ...
Jesus knows.

About Atmosphere Press

Founded in 2015, Atmosphere Press was built on the principles of Honesty, Transparency, Professionalism, Kindness, and Making Your Book Awesome. As an ethical and author-friendly hybrid press, we stay true to that founding mission today.

If you're a reader, enter our giveaway for a free book here:

SCAN TO ENTER
BOOK GIVEAWAY

If you're a writer, submit your manuscript for consideration here:

SCAN TO SUBMIT
MANUSCRIPT

And always feel free to visit Atmosphere Press and our authors online at atmospherepress.com. See you there soon!

About the Author

P.S. GLYCKHERR is now a retired nonprofit professional, ghostwriter, ekphrastic poet and music lyricist. Music and education programs have remained lifelong passions as well as writing poetry about faith, family, friends, and other special people from both the U.S. and around the world. Readers have often commented on the complexities and raw emotion expressed – as well as the lively, unexpected sense of humor found in this author's sizable and diverse body of work.

Milton Keynes UK
Ingram Content Group UK Ltd.
UKHW031303251024
450245UK00004B/320